M.A. Visher
is an instructor
at UCLA
and a consultant
for the Antique Guild

BOOKS IN THE CREATIVE HANDCRAFTS SERIES

THE FINISHING TOUCH

M. A. Visher

Restore, Repair, and Refinish Your Furniture

PRENTICE-HALL, INC., Englewood Cliffs, New Jersey 07632

 A SPECTRUM BOOK

Library of Congress Cataloging in Publication Data

Visher, MA
    The finishing touch.

    (Creative handcrafts series) (A Spectrum Book)
    Includes index.
    1. Furniture—Repairing. 2. Furniture finishing.
I. Title.
TT199.V57   684.1′044   79–22345
ISBN   0–13–317164–7
ISBN   0–13–317156–6 pbk.

Editorial/production supervision by Heath Silberfeld
Art Direction by Jeannette Jacobs
Manufacturing buyers: Cathie Lenard and Barbara Frick
Cover © 1979 by Judith Kazdym Leeds

A SPECTRUM BOOK

© 1980 by Prentice-Hall, Inc., Englewood Cliffs, N.J. 07632

Printed in the United States of America

10 9 8 7 6 5 4 3 2 1

PRENTICE-HALL INTERNATIONAL, INC., *London*
PRENTICE-HALL OF AUSTRALIA PTY. LIMITED, *Sydney*
PRENTICE-HALL OF CANADA, LTD., *Toronto*
PRENTICE-HALL OF INDIA PRIVATE LIMITED, *New Delhi*
PRENTICE-HALL OF JAPAN, INC., *Tokyo*
PRENTICE-HALL OF SOUTHEAST ASIA PTE. LTD., *Singapore*
WHITEHALL BOOKS LIMITED, *Wellington, New Zealand*

This book is lovingly dedicated to my dear friend Carol Bryson

CONTENTS

Introduction 1

1. Restoration of the finish 5

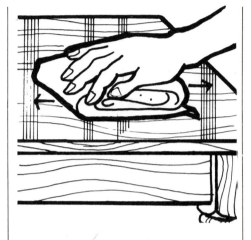

2. Restoration of the surface 19

Contents

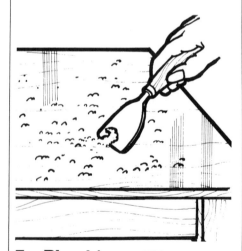

6. Sanding 87

8. Staining 95

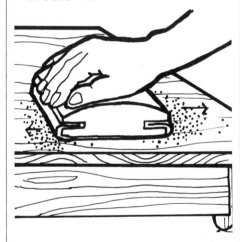

9. Sealing 101

7. New and unpainted or unfinished furniture 91

Contents

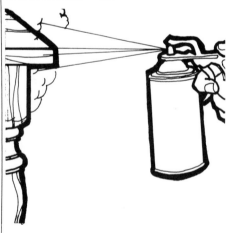

I would like to express my appreciation to all those who helped make this book possible. An extra special thank you goes to Carol Bryson who spent endless hours untangling my sentences so they made sense, who typed, retyped, edited, proofread, and made the experience of writing this book a pleasure. I would like to thank Larry Price who probably taught me most of what I know. Larry, the owner of The Stripper, a very fine furniture restoration shop in Los Angeles, generously allowed me to pick his brain and divulged many of his trade secrets to me. A million thanks to the very clever and talented artists, Rolf Roth and Mario Villamayor, for their creative illustrations which clarify so many steps in the book and for their eternal patience in drawing and redrawing each step. I would also like to thank my daughter Natalie for the help and support she gave to me in completing this project and my students and friends whose endless questions about refinishing inspired me to write this book.

INTRODUCTION

How to use this book

First consult the table of Contents. It lists all the treatments you are likely to use when restoring, repairing, or refinishing furniture. Each chapter covers one area of restoration or refinishing. To help you select a treatment, the first page of each chapter is an explanation of the treatments and the problems which they correct. Each treatment is outlined in the following "recipe" fashion:

Treatment/
Materials/
Directions.

Words in *italics* are defined in the Glossary at the end of the book.

Hints and important points to remember are set in bold type.

Selecting a treatment

RESTORATION VERSUS REFINISHING

Restoration refers to touch-up techniques to repair or remove any flaws in the original finish. Refinishing is a multiprocess operation in which the old finish is removed (stripped), the piece is repaired, then *stained*, *sealed*, and covered with a new finish coat.

Restoring has many advantages over refinishing. It's usually easier and less time-consuming than refinishing, and because it requires fewer materials it's also cheaper. Most important, *restoring* leaves intact the wood's *patina* (color changes caused by aging), thus increasing the value of the furniture and enhancing its beauty. Generally, removing the original *finish* decreases the value of an antique.

With a very old piece of furniture that may be of great value, it's best to have it appraised before starting any treatment. There are times when *restoration* is impossible—the original *finish* may be crumbling and flaking or it may have been painted or *varnished* over, or it may have had a poor finish to begin with—and then a new finish will be an improvement.

The decision to restore or refinish is entirely up to you. *Your own opinion* about the result you want is all that matters. Most furniture is bought to be used and enjoyed, not as an investment. If you hate the color or finish, you're better off changing it to what you'll be happy with.

Why I wrote this book

In my classes on furniture care and repair, I always ask my students why they're taking the class. One man spoke for the majority when he wrote:

I have a house full of old furniture I bought at swap meets, garage sales, thrift stores, Goodwill and the Salvation Army. At the time they looked like they had potential. Some of them are even antiques. I started to do something to each piece. None of them are finished, so I turned them all against the walls so nobody would notice. Now I'm running out of walls!

I realized that these people weren't just procrastinating or lacking a Saturday morning all to themselves, but that most of the books on furniture refinishing require extensive reading before the do-it-yourselfer can get down to the fun part with a brush and some sandpaper. I have created a bare-bones, easy-to-follow, technically sound manual based on my years of enjoyable experience in making old furniture beautiful.

My directions for any single treatment are self-contained in each section. It is not necessary to read the whole book before getting down to the fun of it.

Sources

Most materials required in this book are available through hardware stores; some are not. Specialty and unusual items not carried by hardware stores are indicated in the list of Sources at the end of the book. For widely available products, the type of store that carries them is listed. If a product is made by only one company, that company's name and address is listed along with the type of stores that might carry its product.

Introduction

1. RESTORATION OF THE FINISH

The *finish* is a coating (generally lacquer) which covers the surface of the wood. It serves to protect and enhance the wood's natural beauty. The finish can be *high-gloss* (very shiny), *semigloss* or *satin* (medium lustre), or *flat* (low lustre).

Five methods of *restoration* of the finish are outlined below. The method you choose depends on the problems you have and the results you want. Using the following chart, pick the treatment, and you'll find the complete directions on the given page.

A word about cleaning: Cleaning is the first step in many of the treatments in this book. Whenever cleaning is suggested, use the basic instructions on page 6.

CLEANING

Cleaning is the first step in many processes in this book. Whenever cleaning is indicated, just follow the steps below:

PROBLEM	TREATMENT	RESULT
Original finish is in good shape but covered with layers of dirt.	Cleaning (page 6)	Old *patina* and original *finish* are visible.
Finish is worn and dull.	Paste-waxing (page 10)	Restores lustre to the finish.
Scratches, discoloration, white spots.	Scrub and restain (page 12)	Scratches disappear; finish and color are even.
Scratches, white spots.	Howard's Restor-a-finish* (page 14)	Scratches are camouflaged; white rings disappear.
Finish worn in spots.	Finish over existing finish (page 16)	*Finish* is uniform; worn spots, small scratches disappear.

*Howard's Restor-a-Finish: I'm not making any sales pitches for brand products, but I will mention them if they are exceptionally effective or unique (or if I own stock in the company).

MATERIALS

Soft cloths

Paint thinner

Steel wool

Soft brush
(toothbrush or nailbrush)

Container for thinner
(jar or coffee can)

1. Pour 1 cup of paint thinner into container.

2. Dip the cloth in the thinner and apply to the furniture.

3. Rub off the dirt with a clean cloth. Always rub in the direction of the grain of the wood.

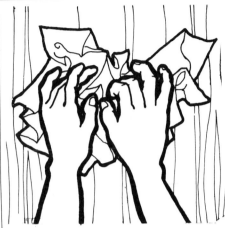

Paint thinner dissolves dirt, wax, and polish. IT WILL NOT DISSOLVE THE FINISH! The dissolved dirt and wax become gooey, and it looks like you're wiping off the finish. Don't worry! You're only removing the "waxy build-up" and residue on top of the finish.

FOR BUILT-UP DIRT

1. Apply paint thinner liberally with a brush and allow to set for 2 to 3 minutes.

2. Rub off the dirt with steel wool. **If the finish is high-gloss, don't use steel wool—use a cloth instead.**

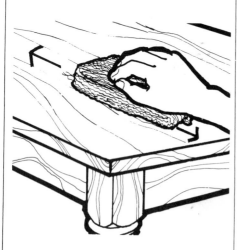

FOR CARVED AREAS

1. Brush on thinner with a paint brush and allow to set for 2 or 3 minutes.

2. Scrub off the dirt with a toothbrush or nailbrush.

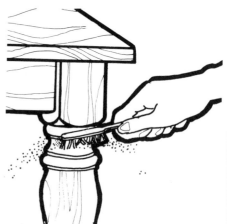

3. Wipe off excess thinner with a clean cloth.

After an hour, when the wood has thoroughly dried, the finish may appear somewhat dull. If you don't have to use one of the other treatments to get rid of spots and scratches, you can bring up the lustre again by simply paste-waxing (page 10) or by applying another coat of *finish* (page 16).

PASTE-WAXING

Paste-waxing protects the furniture's *finish* and produces lustre in the wood. It's like polishing shoes.

MATERIALS

Soft cloths
Steel wool (grade 0000)
Paste wax
(any brand *without* silicone)

1. Apply a coat of paste wax to the surface of the wood using steel wool or a cloth if the finish is *high-gloss.*

2. Allow the paste wax to dry—approximately 15 minutes.

3. Buff with a soft cloth until the wood shines. Buff in the direction of the wood grain.

Drying time will vary depending on the humidity. Test a small area before tackling the entire piece. If your cloth drags when you start to buff, the wax is not dry enough. If you have to rub long and hard to produce a shine, you've waited too long. Confine your waxing to small areas (a couple square feet at a time). Trying to wax the entire piece at once results in some areas drying too hard. If this happens to you, don't worry! Just keep rubbing. A lot of elbow grease will eventually buff off the hardened wax, creating a great shine. Or you can soften the hardened wax by wiping with a cloth and some paint thinner.

Paste-waxing

SCRUB AND RESTAIN

The scrubbing and restaining treatment camouflages scratches, white spots, and discolorations and makes the color even.

MATERIALS

Soft cloths

Paint thinner

Steel wool (grade 0000)*

Paint brush

Oil-base stain
(color should match wood)

*If the existing finish is high-gloss, don't use steel wool—it will dull the mirrorlike shine. Use a cloth instead.

1. Clean the entire piece of furniture. (See cleaning, p. 6.) Wipe the wood dry with a cloth.

2. Shake the can of stain to mix the contents.

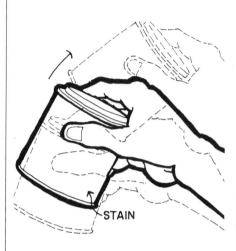

3. Apply the stain evenly with a paint brush.

4. Use the steel wool (or a cloth if the finish is high-gloss) to rub the stain into the surface. *Always rub with the grain of the wood.*

5. Wipe off the excess stain with a clean cloth.

6. Allow to dry overnight (24 hours). (Actually a night isn't 24 hours, but it would be nice if some of them were.)

Now to bring up the lustre, apply a coat of paste wax (page 10), or if you're really ambitious, apply another coat of finish (page 16).

HOWARD'S RESTOR-A-FINISH

Howard's Restor-a-Finish is a kind of camouflaging stain that completely removes white spots, covers scratches, and revives "cloudy" *finishes*.

MATERIALS

Soft cloths

Paint thinner

Steel wool (grade 0000)

Howard's Restor-a-Finish (color should match the wood)

1. Pour a small amount of Restor-a-Finish onto the steel wool—or a cloth if the finish is high-gloss—and apply a thin, even coat to the wood. **Don't pour it directly on the surface!**

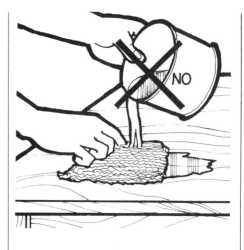

2. Apply the Restor-a-Finish to the surface by rubbing with the grain in long, even strokes.

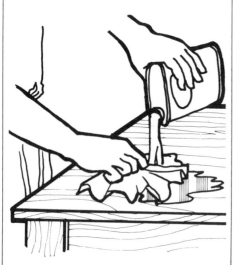

14

3. Wipe off the excess Restor-a-Finish with a clean cloth.

4. Allow to dry overnight (24 hours).

Now to bring up the lustre, apply a coat of paste wax (page 10), or if you're really ambitious, apply another coat of finish (page 16).

FINISH OVER AN EXISTING FINISH

You can spruce up a worn finish by adding a top coat of lacquer over the original coats of finish. It's an excellent *restoration* technique, and it preserves the *patina* of the wood because you don't strip off the old finish.

MATERIALS

Soft cloths

Paint thinner

1 can spray lacquer (in *high-gloss, medium,* or *semi-gloss* as desired)

Wet/dry sandpaper (grade 400 silicone carbide sandpaper)

Tack rag

1. Clean the entire piece of furniture thoroughly. (See cleaning, page 6.)

2. Sand the entire surface with wet/dry sandpaper. The light abrasive action prepares the surface to receive lacquer.

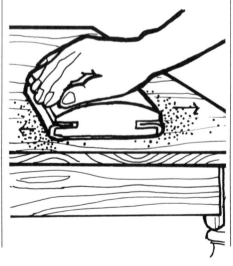

3. Wipe the surface with cloths, then wipe again with the tack rag to remove all sawdust and dirt.

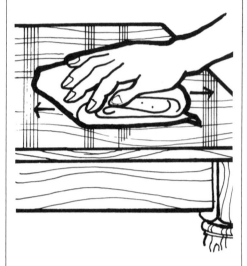

4. Shake the spray can vigorously.

5. Check the can's nozzle by spraying in the air—you should get a fine mist of spray.

6. Apply a very thin coat of lacquer by spraying with an even, circular motion.

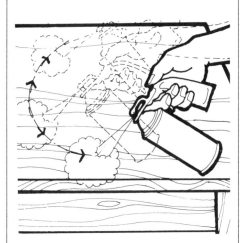

7. After spraying, clear the nozzle by turning the can upside-down and depressing the spray valve until it is cleared of all spray and only air comes out. This prevents the nozzle from clogging.

8. Allow to dry overnight (24 hours).

To add a hand-rubbed look, you may want to finish up with a coat of wax (page 10).

2. RESTORATION OF THE SURFACE

YOUR PROBLEM	MY REMEDY
Spots	Touch-up/or paint-out (page 21)
Minor scratches	Fill with wax (page 24)
Deep scratches, holes, gouges, cigarette burns	Fill with hard wax or *wood putty*, and paint out (hard wax, page 26; wood putty, page 29)
Large holes or gouges	Wood block insert (page 32)
Veneer blister, loose *veneer*, missing *veneer*, missing *inlay*	Match veneer or inlay and reglue (loose *veneer* or *inlay*, page 35; missing *veneer*, page 37; *veneer* blister, page 40.)

SELECTING A TECHNIQUE

Sometimes it's necessary to do repairs on the surface of the wood. Spots, scratches, holes, cigarette burns, gouges, *veneer* blisters, missing or loose *inlay* or *veneer* are problems which frequently need attention. The table above lists each problem separately with an easy remedy.

SPOT TOUCH-UP OR PAINT-OUT TECHNIQUE

The touch-up (or paint-out) method is used to camouflage any kind of imperfections on the surface. In painting out you're actually copying or "faking" the grain of the wood using *acrylic paints*. If you're wondering, "Can this be used to fix up the spot where I left a paint can on the table I just refinished?" the answer is yes—paint-out technique will disguise any spots you goofed up on the surface. Painting out is the last step in many of the surface repairs outlined in later chapters.

MATERIALS

Small set of *acrylic paints* that includes these colors: raw umber, raw sienna, burnt umber, burnt sienna, black, and white.
By mixing these colors you can match any wood color.

Several fine-pointed artist's paint brushes

Steel wool (grade 0000)

Wet/dry sandpaper (grade 400)

1. Study the grain of the wood. With your paints you'll be duplicating the lighter background and the darker grain lines. Sand the spot with grade-400 wet/dry sandpaper.

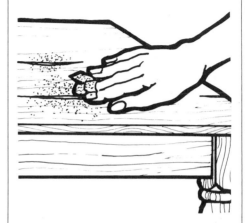

2. Mix the acrylic paints together to match the background (lighter) color of the wood. You need only mix about ¼ teaspoon of paint.

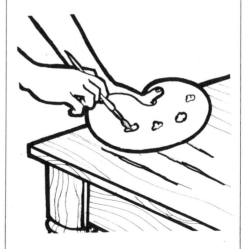

21

3. Using a dry, fine-pointed brush, paint this mixture lightly over the spot. It's better to build the color on gradually with feathered, successive strokes than to paint it on thickly.

4. Allow the paint to dry and sand lightly with grade-0000 steel wool.

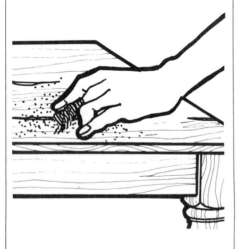

5. Study the existing grain of the wood. (A magnifying glass will help you to see the grain more clearly.) Try to duplicate the grain lines over the first coat of background color by painting with the darker color. Use a very-fine-pointed brush to paint the grain lines.

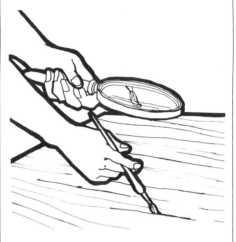

6. Allow the grain lines to dry (about 1 hour), and lightly sand with grade 0000 steel wool.

22

7. Seal the paint-out with a light coat of lacquer.

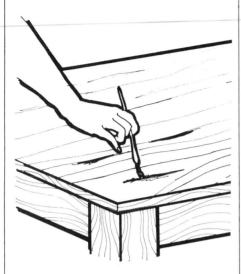

8. Let dry for 1 hour.

9. With the grade 0000 steel wool lightly rub out any difference in the fresh lacquer and the lacquer on the rest of the piece.

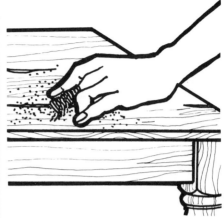

The secret of the paint-out technique is using a practically dry brush. Dip the brush in paint and then brush it on a scrap of paper until all you get is a light outline of color.

REPAIRING MINOR SCRATCHES

Soft wax sticks or crayons can be used for very small holes (up to ⅛″ across). (For larger holes or gouges, see repairing holes, gouges, scratches, cigarette burns with hard wax, p. 26.)

MATERIALS

Large box of crayons
with several shades of brown
or
soft *wax sticks* for scratch repair
(sold in hardware stores).
Soft wax sticks can be
rubbed directly into the scratch;
they do not need to be melted.

Shellac

Flat-edged knife (small putty knife)

Steel wool (grade 0000)

1. Select the crayon which most nearly matches the color of the wood. (You can melt two or three and mix them to match the wood color exactly.)

2. Rub the wax into the scratch, using the flat-edged knife to pack it in smoothly. The wax is soft—use your finger to smooth it out.

3. Paint crayon or wax patch with a coat of shellac.

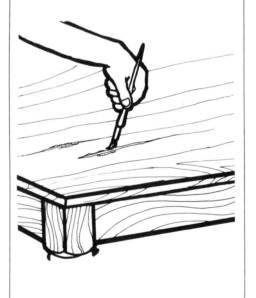

4. After 1 hour, when the shellac is dry, rub the surface very lightly with grade 0000 steel wool, rubbing with the grain, to tone down the excess gloss.

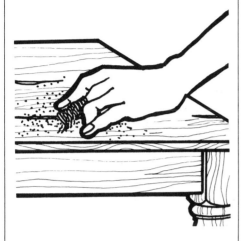

Shellac should be purchased in small quantities because it spoils. Once opened, shellac absorbs moisture from the air and will dry cloudy. Always use a new container of shellac.

REPAIR OF HOLES, GOUGES, SCRATCHES, AND CIGARETTE BURNS WITH HARD WAX

Hard wax can be used to fill small holes and gouges up to ½″ across. *Wax sticks* are sold in most hardware stores in wood *stain* colors. Get the color that matches the wood you're repairing. Make sure your shellac is fresh, too!

MATERIALS

Hard-*wax sticks*

Flat-bladed knife
(small putty knife)

Wet/dry sandpaper (grade 400)

Shellac

Shellac is the only finish that sticks to wax. It can be painted over with lacquer, acrylic paint, oil-base paint, varnish, or polyurethane. Shellac spoils— always use a new container.

Heat source
(Sterno or a gas burner)

1. Prepare the gouge or hole by digging out any loose pieces or burnt portions.

2. Lightly sand the edges of the hole with grade 400 wet/dry sandpaper.

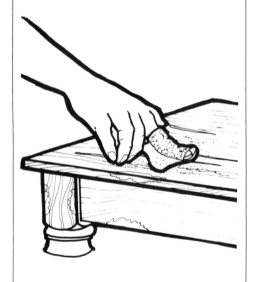

3. Fill the hole with wax. (If necessary, two colors can be melted and mixed together.) To melt the wax, heat the knife over a flame. When the blade is hot, hold it over the hole and press the wax on the blade, letting it drip until the hole is full.

4. With the flat of the knife, smooth the surface and pack the wax into the hole. When the hole is filled up to the level of the surface, smooth the wax with the knife.

5. Let the wax harden for 5 minutes. Lightly sand it level with grade 400 wet/dry sandpaper.

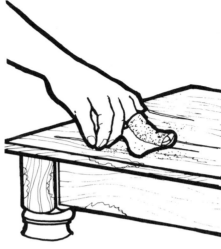

6. Paint the wax fill with a coat of shellac.

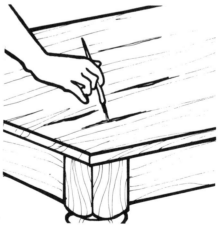

Wax must be sealed with shellac before applying anything else to the surface.

7. When the shellac is dry (about 1 hour), rub it out gently with grade-0000 steel wool.

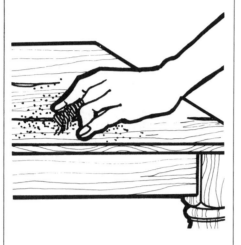

If necessary, paint out the wax fill as described on page 21. If the repair is obvious, it should be painted out. If you are not satisfied with the wax fill, dig out the wax and start over again. The process can be repeated over and over again.

REPAIR OF HOLES, GOUGES,
SCRATCHES, AND CIGARETTE BURNS
WITH WOOD PUTTY

Wood putty (wood dough, plastic
wood) can be used to fill small
holes and gouges up to 1″ across.
Any larger hole should be filled
with a wood patch (see repairing
large holes, page 32), because wood
putty will shrink and fall out. Buy
the wood putty to match the wood,
or buy plain putty, in powder form,
and mix it with *oil paint, UTC
color,* or *stain* to match the color of
the wood.

MATERIALS

Wet/dry sandpaper

Wood putty

Sharp knife or needle

Acetone
(fingernail polish remover will do)

Flat-edged knife
(small putty knife)

1. Prepare the gouge or hole by
digging out any loose pieces or
burnt portions.

2. Lightly sand the edges of the
hole with wet/dry sandpaper.

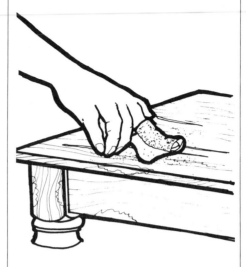

3. Take out a small amount of wood
putty (¼ to ½ teaspoon) and close
the putty can immediately to
prevent evaporation.

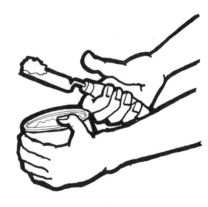

Repairs with wood putty

29

The solvent for most brands of wood putty is acetone, which rapidly evaporates, leaving the putty hard and useless. It can, however, be softened by adding more acetone (fingernail polish remover) to make it the consistency of wet modeling clay. Check the directions on your can of solvent.

4. Pack a small amount of putty in the hole using your finger or a putty knife.

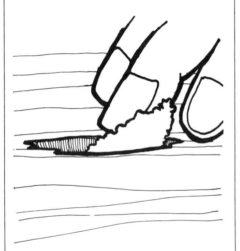

5. Let the first layer dry (½ hour or so), and pack in a second layer.

6. When this is dry, repeat the layering until the hole is level with the surface. Packing putty too thickly or filling the hole all at once will result in shrinkage.

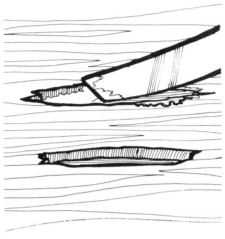

If needed, paint out the fill to camouflage it. (See spot touch-up, or paint-out, page 21.) Painting-out should only be done if the putty patch is really noticeable.

HARD WAX VERSUS PUTTY FOR FILLING GOUGES

Hard wax nearly always must be painted-out. *Wood putty* has to be painted-out only when it is used to fill a large hole, or if the color of the putty doesn't match the wood. Sometimes putty will shrink after it has dried and separate from the edge of the hole. Even hard wax is much softer than putty and should be used on holes less than ½" across. Both the wood putty and wax filling processes take about the same amount of time and require equal effort, so you might try both methods and use the one that's easier for you.

REPAIRING LARGE HOLES WITH A
WOODEN BLOCK

The wood block technique should
be used for repairing any hole larger
than 1″ across.

MATERIALS

Sharp paring knife

Block of wood to match
the piece being repaired

White glue

Rubber mallet

Small wood saw

Electric or hand drill

Wax paper

Stack of books (for weight)

Sandpaper (grades 280 and 400)

1. Use the paring knife to square off
the hole so that the sides slope in
toward the bottom. (See illustration.)

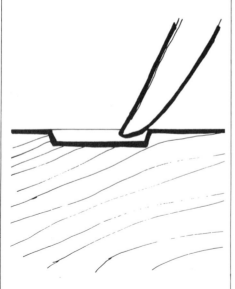

2. Drill a small hole in the bottom
of the hole. This will allow the
excess glue to escape.

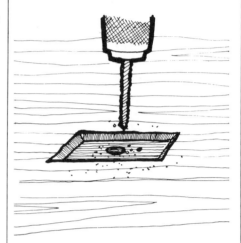

3. Clean out the drilled hole by
scraping away loose particles of
wood with the knife.

4. With the small wood saw cut a wood block larger than the hole. Cut the sides at an angle so the block will fit in the hole. (See illustration.) Gently ease the block into the hole to test the fit. If it doesn't fit, sand it down.

5. Apply glue to all surfaces of the hole and the bottom surfaces of the wood block.

6. Pound the block into the hole using the rubber mallet. Wipe off the excess glue.

7. Allow the repair to dry under pressure for 24 hours: put a sheet of wax paper and a stack of books on top of the block of wood.

Repairing large holes

8. Sand the block smooth and flush to the surface using wet/dry sandpaper (grade 280). Sand until surface is very smooth using wet/dry sandpaper (grade 400). Stain and camouflage the block insert by painting-out. (See touch-up or painting-out, page 21.)

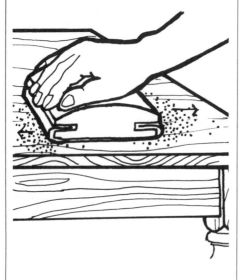

REPAIRING LOOSE INLAY AND VENEER

Inlay is the term used for decorative patterns of small wood pieces set into the surface of a piece of furniture; it is also called marquetry and parquetry. Marquetry is fashioned in floral patterns, and parquetry is geometrical. The inlay is cemented into the surface with glue.

Veneer is a thin surface layer of wood ($1/64$ to $1/32$ " thickness), usually of a finer quality than the base wood.

Look over the rules for gluing (page 44) before you start on this repair.

MATERIALS

Knife

Straight edge

Soft *wax* (crayon)
in color matching wood

White *glue*

Wax paper

Stack of books (for weight)

1. Remove the old veneer or inlay by prying it up with the knife blade. You may have to break it off. Don't worry if it breaks off unevenly—the irregular line will make the repair less noticeable.

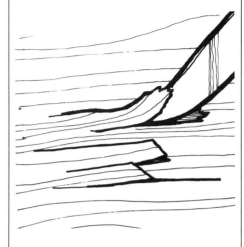

2. Scrape off the old glue with the knife blade.

3. Reglue the loose piece of veneer or inlay and allow it to dry under pressure for 24 hours.

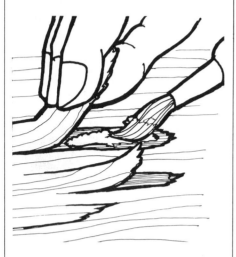

4. To create pressure, cover the repair area with a sheet of wax paper to prevent sticking, and stack about twenty heavy books (heavy in weight, that is) on top of the wax paper.

5. If there are cracks around the repaired area, fill them with matching crayon wax. Follow directions under repairing minor scratches, page 24.

6. Paste-wax the entire area after the glue is dry. (See paste-waxing, page 10.)

REPAIRING MISSING INLAY AND VENEER

Inlay refers to decorative patterns of small pieces of wood set into the surface of the base wood; it is also called marquetry and parquetry. Marquetry is fashioned in floral patterns, and parquetry is geometrical. Inlay is bonded to the base wood with glue.

Veneer is a thin surface layer of wood ($1/64$ to $1/32$ "inch" thick), usually of a finer quality than the base wood it's glued to.

Check over the rules for gluing (page 44) before starting on the inlay or veneer repair. Also, if you can't use a patch piece from some inconspicuous part of the furniture, cut a piece from a matching sheet of veneer. Sheets of veneer are sold by better lumberyards (also see Sources, p. 133). It's impossible to match exactly, so just look for a piece similar in color and grain pattern. Select a veneer which when wet matches the color you want, and stain and finish it before cutting (see staining, p. 96 and finishes, page 110).

MATERIALS

White *glue*
Single-edged razor blades
Wax paper
Piece of matching *veneer* or *inlay*
Stack of books (for weight)
Wax paper

1. Trim the edges around the area of the missing veneer so that there are no jagged edges.

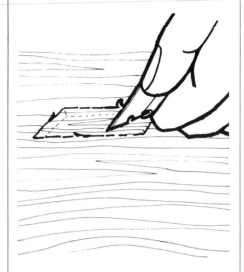

2. With a razor blade, cut a piece of veneer in the shape of the missing section. Do this by tracing the shape of the missing section on thin paper, then transferring it onto the sheet of veneer using carbon paper underneath.

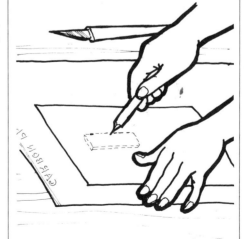

3. If the veneer is too thick for the hole you are filling or the piece you're replacing, either scrape out the hole more or sand the underside of the veneer using a medium-grade (200) *garnet paper* wrapped around a *sanding block*. (See sanding, page 88.)

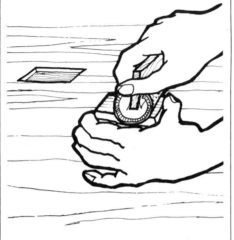

4. Apply glue to the back of the veneer and to the surface being patched.

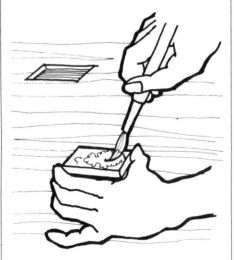

5. Press the piece of veneer in place. Wipe off the excess glue.

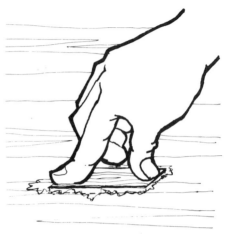

6. Cover the area with wax paper, apply weight (a high stack of books), and allow the glue to dry for 24 hours.

7. Touch up the area where the two veneers meet. (See spot touch-up or paint-out, page 21.)

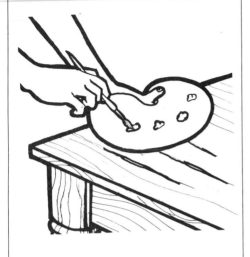

REPAIRING VENEER BLISTERS

Veneer is a thin surface layer of wood ($\frac{1}{64}$ to $\frac{1}{32}$ ″ thickness), usually of a finer quality than the base wood it's glued to. Blisters in the *veneer* are caused by moisture under the surface that expands with an increase in air temperature.

Look over the rules for gluing (page 44) before you start on this repair.

MATERIALS

Single-edge razor blade

White *glue*

Dishtowel

Iron

Glue syringe (see list
of sources for where to find one)

or

Regular syringe

Wax paper

Stack of books (for weight)

1. With the razor blade, slit the blister along the grain. The slit should be the entire length of the blister.

2. Using a glue syringe or a regular syringe, shoot some glue under each flap of the blister.

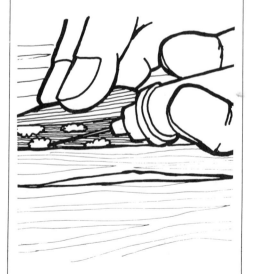

3. Place a piece of waxed paper on top of the blister, and on top of that put a dishtowel folded in three or four layers.

4. Apply an iron on medium heat, pressing down firmly. Be sure the dishtowel is big enough to cover the bottom of the iron. The sliced edges of the veneer will flatten and overlap.

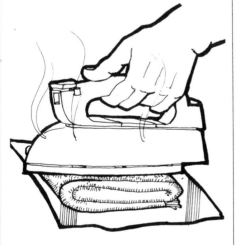

5. Very carefully slice off the part of the top section that has overlapped. Wipe off the excess glue.

6. Apply the iron again until the veneer is flat.

7. Put a stack of books on the repair, and let it dry for 24 hours.

3. STRUCTURAL REPAIRS

RULES FOR GLUING

Gluing may seem like a temporary means of repair, but it is actually one of the most frequently used methods of bonding in permanent furniture construction and repair. Moldings and decorative trims are attached with *glue*, and gluing effectively cements joints where two or more parts meet (such as in the dovetails of drawers and in the joints of arms and legs).

Avoid using nails and screws to repair furniture—they will eventually work loose. Use *white glue*, such as Elmer's, Wilhold, Weldwood, or Glubird, whenever possible.

1. Clean old glue from the surface before regluing by scraping it off with a knife.

2. Apply glue to both surfaces to be bonded. Let the glue soak in for about 5 minutes before joining surfaces together. Wipe off the excess glue.

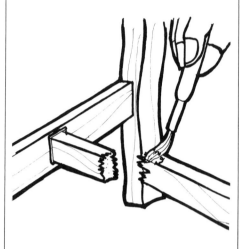

3. The repair must dry under pressure. Use clamps, tape, rope, a stack of books, or whatever to apply pressure, and let the glue dry for at least 24 hours.

Glue that can't be scraped off can be softened by applying hot vinegar. Heat the vinegar, soak cotton balls in it, and apply them to the old glue until it softens.

What if you glue something together and it comes out crooked? I would probably leave it that way—after all, nobody's perfect. But if it's really awful, you can remove the glue with hot vinegar and cotton balls, and start over.

IDEAS FOR CLAMPING

Glue should always dry under pressure. Clamps are used to apply pressure. Many types of clamps are available. If you will be doing a lot of repairs, it will be worth the investment to purchase a set of clamps in many sizes. Several pairs of C-clamps, an encyclopedia set (for weight), and a rope are sufficient for doing an occasional structural repair.

SOME TIPS ON CLAMPING

1. Never place the clamp directly on the furniture. Place a flat board between the clamp and furniture. This will prevent the clamp from gouging the furniture by spreading the pressure uniformly across the area being glued.

2. Place a piece of wax paper or tinfoil between the furniture and the flat board or books or whatever you use to apply pressure. Any glue forced out by the pressure will stick to the paper, preventing the flat board from being glued to the furniture. The paper can easily be scraped off the furniture.

3. Heavy books, such as encyclopedias, are excellent sources of pressure when used as weights in applying pressure to flat surfaces.

TOURNIQUET METHOD

A rope can be used to apply pressure. Tie the rope around the parts being glued. Tuck thick folds of fabric (a dishtowel or a washcloth folded several times is perfect) under the rope at each corner to prevent the rope from gouging the furniture. Apply pressure by using a stick or dowel in a tourniquet fashion.

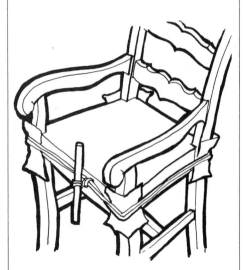

VISE METHOD

Create a vise using flat boards and C-clamps. To create pressure when gluing a flat surface, put a board across the top and another board across the bottom of the surface. Use C-clamps at each end of the boards to create pressure.

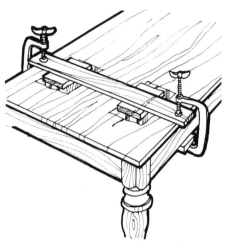

REPAIRING LOOSE JOINTS

A leg, stretcher, or rung that is loose (wiggles) in the joint can be remedied with gluing. If the joint is enlarged, though, and the piece is falling out, you'll have to do a heavier repair. (See mortises, page 50.) Before getting tangled up in the following directions, look over the rules for gluing (page 44).

MATERIALS

Sharp paring knife

White *glue*

Clamps

Cloth or wood shims
(wooden slivers or toothpicks)

Take the piece apart if you think you can put it back together again.

1. With the paring knife, scrape off the old glue. If the glue is really hardened, soften it by applying cotton soaked in hot vinegar.

2. Fill the excess space in the hole with cloth or wood shims.

3. Apply glue to the surfaces to be joined, and clamp them together.

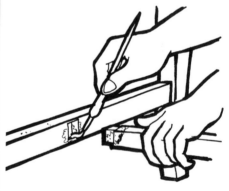

4. Let dry for 24 hours.

If you can't take the piece apart, you will need a glue syringe (see list of sources for where to get one) or a regular hypodermic syringe to make the following repair:

1. Fill the syringe with white glue and shoot the glue into the loose joint.

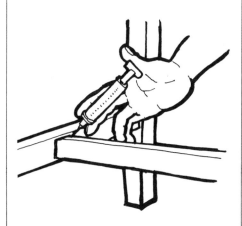

2. Apply the clamps and let the repair dry under pressure for 24 hours.

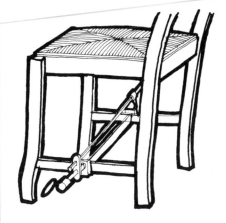

To keep the syringe from clogging between uses, store it in a large jar full of water.

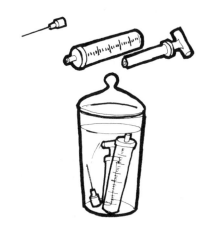

REPAIRING OVERSIZED SOCKETS (MORTISES)

Often the arm, leg, or stretcher has worked away from the joint and the socket is too wide to hold it. This is corrected by filling the oversized socket with a wooden plug and then drilling a new hole.

MATERIALS

Dowel—same diameter as hole to be filled

White *glue*

Electric drill

C-clamps

Small paint brush

1. Make a plug by cutting a piece from a dowel the same diameter as the hole.

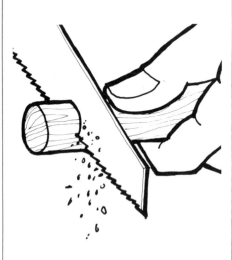

2. Apply glue to all surfaces of the socket and to the bottom and circumference of the dowel plug. Insert the dowel plug.

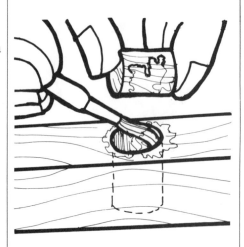

3. Clamp the plug and allow the glue to dry for 24 hours.

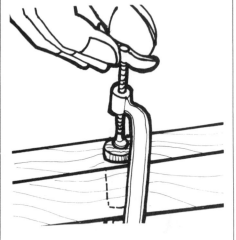

4. Sand the dowel flush with the surface.

5. Drill a new hole in the plug. The hole should be the same diameter as the piece which fits into it.

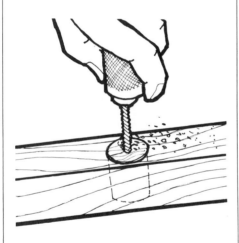

6. With the paint brush, apply glue to the piece and to the new socket. Insert the piece into the new socket.

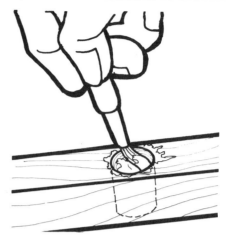

7. Clamp and allow to dry for 24 hours.

REPAIRING BROKEN LIMBS (ARMS, LEGS, POSTS, STRETCHERS, RUNGS, ETC.)

Don't throw away a table or chair just because the arm or leg has been broken off. Restoring it by the following method will make it sturdier than it was originally.

Look over the rules for gluing (page 44). If the piece of furniture must support weight, follow the procedure for reinforcing broken limbs (page 54).

MATERIALS

Sharp paring knife

White *glue*

Clamps

Small paint brush

1. Remove the broken limb from the joint. Scrape off all the old glue with the knife.

2. Use a small brush to apply glue to the break.

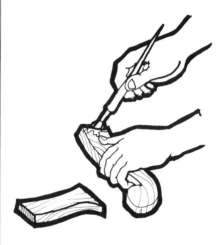

3. Clamp at the break and allow to dry for 24 hours.

4. Reglue the arm or missing limb, and clamp.

5. Allow to dry for 24 hours.

REINFORCING BROKEN LIMBS (LEGS, ARMS, STRETCHERS, RUNGS, POSTS, ETC.)

If the broken limb supports a lot of weight, strengthen it by placing a dowel inside the broken limb. Read the rules for gluing (page 44) before you tackle this one.

MATERIALS

Sharp paring knife

White *glue*

Wooden *dowel*—smaller diameter than broken limb

Clamps

Electric or hand drill

1. Drill a hole the size of the dowel in both sides of the break in the limb. The hole is drilled into the center core of the limb.

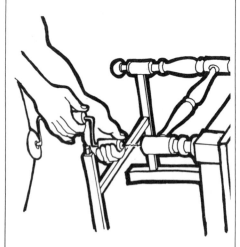

2. Apply glue to the hole.

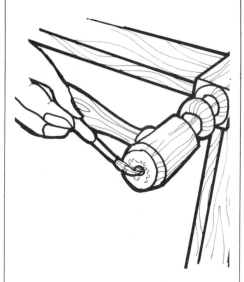

3. Glue the dowel into the hole and glue the break.

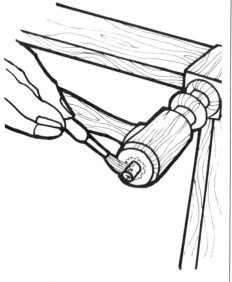

4. Clamp the repair.

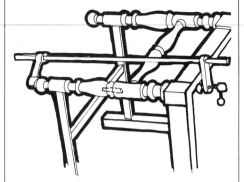

5. Allow to dry for 24 hours.

REPAIRING LOOSE SCREWS

Screws often work loose from wood due to friction from use. Better furniture is not put together with screws but with wooden dowels glued in place. But if you have a "screw loose," this remedy will enable you to "get it together." You might look over rules for gluing (page 44) before you start this process.

MATERIALS

Screwdriver
White *glue*
Shims
(toothpicks, matchsticks, or fabric)
Small paring knife

1. Remove the screw.

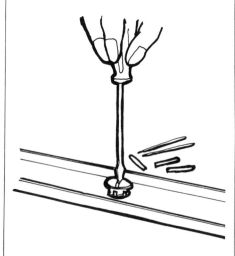

2. Scrape out the screw hole.

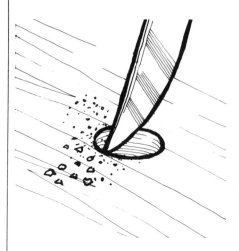

3. Plug the opening with shims (matchsticks, toothpicks, or fabric—whatever works best). Apply the glue.

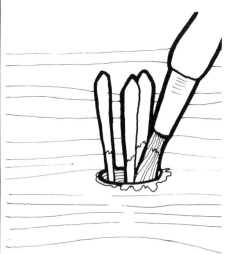

4. Replace the screw while the glue is still wet. Trim away any portion of the shims that show.

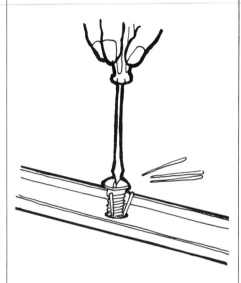

If the screw hole is too large to fill with shims, fill the hole with a piece of dowel and replace the screw. See repairing oversized sockets (page 50).

REPAIRING A SMALL SPLIT

Dampness and drying can cause panels to split. If the split has not gone completely through the panel it can be repaired with *wood putty*. (See the section on repairing holes with wood putty, page 29.) The following procedure can be used to glue panels that have split all the way.

MATERIALS

White glue

Wet/dry sandpaper (grade 400)

Duct tape or adhesive tape

Wood splines
(slivers or splinters of wood—same kind as the section being repaired)

or

Wood putty in color matching wood in panel

Broad knife

1. If the split panel moves freely within the frame, force the panel back together while still in the frame and glue it together. Stick a broad knife between the frame and the panel to shift both sides of the split panel together.

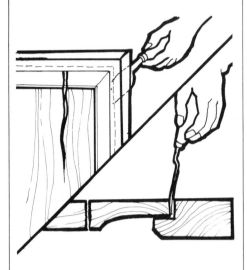

2. Use duct tape or adhesive tape to hold it together while the glue dries.

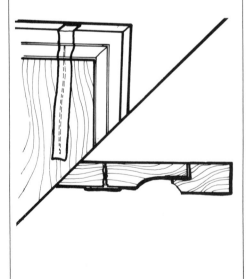

3. When the glue is dry, remove the tape from the side of the panel that is visible. Leave the tape on the backside of the panel for reinforcement.

4. Fill any gaps with matching wood splines or wood putty. Wedge the splines into the gap and glue. (If you use wood putty, see the section on filling, page 29.)

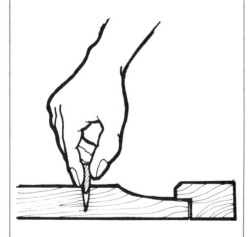

5. Sand with grade 400 wet/dry sandpaper, sanding with the grain of the wood.

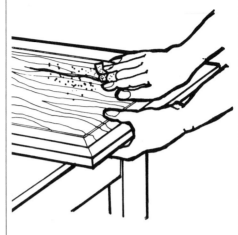

If necessary, touch up the repair to camouflage the split. (See spot touch-up or paint-out, page 21.)

REPAIRING A LARGE SPLIT

When the split is too wide to be forced back together and glued, it is necessary to fill the split with matching pieces of wood.

MATERIALS

Wood *splines*
(slivers or wedges of matching wood)
White *glue*
Clamps

1. Cut matching pieces of wood the size of the split. Apply glue to the split.

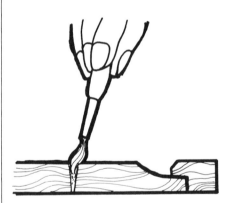

2. Insert the wood pieces into the split.

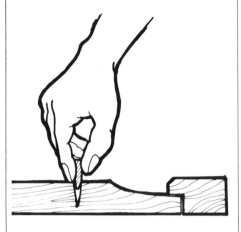

3. Glue and clamp. Let dry for 24 hours.

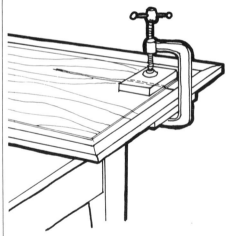

4. Reinforce the back by gluing small blocks of wood along the split.

REPAIRING STICKING DRAWERS

Sticking drawers are caused by warping. Drawers that stick or don't slide at all can be repaired by one of the following methods.
Try this first:

MATERIALS

Wax (an old candle is perfect)

1. Rub the candle or a piece of wax along the sides, bottom, and at any point the drawer is sticking.

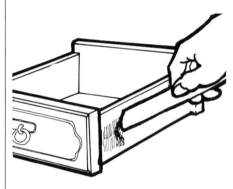

If that doesn't work:

MATERIALS

Wet/dry sandpaper (grade 280)

1. Examine the drawer to see where it is sticking. Look for shiny areas caused by friction.

2. Sand down the rough areas using sandpaper until the drawer will move smoothly again.

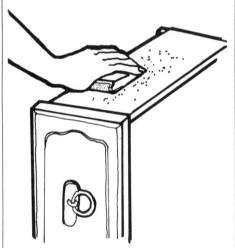

DRAWERS THAT DON'T CLOSE FLUSH

Drawers that do not close flush with their case, stick out, or are recessed when closed are caused by a missing or misplaced drawer stop.

MATERIALS

White glue

C-clamp

Small block of wood (approximately ½ × ½ × 2″)

Chisel

1. Remove the small block of wood in the drawer opening that stops the drawer when it's pushed into the case. (These blocks may be at the front, the back, or along the sides of the drawer opening.) If there are no blocks you will have to replace them. To determine the correct size, duplicate the drawer stops in another drawer. If there is only one drawer, you'll have to guess the size of the stops.

2. Glue the drawer stops into the bottom of the opening of the drawer case. Glue them at the point the drawer should stop to be flush with the case.*

3. Use a C-clamp to hold drawer stops in place and under pressure while the glue dries.

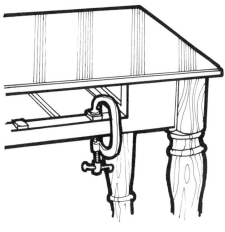

* This point can be determined by the thickness of the drawer's front panel. If it's 1″ thick, set the stops 1″ back.

4. Allow to dry for 24 hours.

DRAWERS THAT ARE NOT LEVEL

Drawers that are not level must be lifted to close or open or fall down into the case. This problem is caused by worn or missing drawer glides.

Worn Glides

MATERIALS

Wood putty
Wet/dry sandpaper (grade 400)
Flat-edged knife

1. Inspect the drawer glides for worn spots.

2. Fill any gouges in the glides with wood putty following the directions on repairing holes with wood putty, page 29.

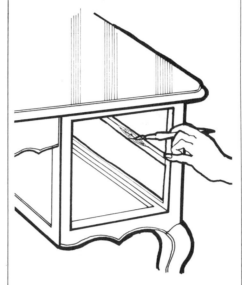

Missing Glides

MATERIALS

Small boards

1. If glide is missing or beyond repair, replace it. Duplicate the drawer glide using the glide in another drawer as a guide.

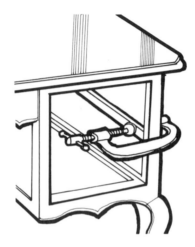

2. Glue the glide in place. Allow to dry 24 hours.

DRAWERS THAT ARE FALLING APART

Drawers are usually joined at the corners in dovetail joints. When these dovetails loosen or become unglued, the drawer falls apart.

MATERIALS

White *glue*
Duct *tape*

1. Clean and scrape off the old glue.

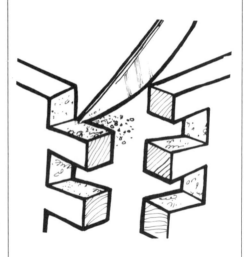

2. Apply glue to all dovetail surfaces that meet.

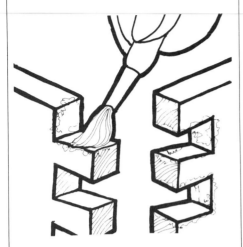

3. Reassemble the drawers.

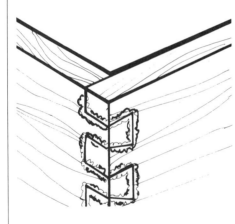

4. Wipe off the excess glue.

5. Clamp the drawer using duct tape.

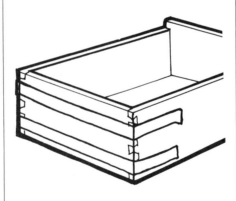

6. Replace the drawer in the case to dry, so that it dries to fit the shape of the cavity. Make sure the excess glue is wiped off before you put the drawer in.

REPLACING MISSING PARTS

When a part of a piece of furniture such as molding, beading, a stretcher, spindles, or a decorative part is missing or broken beyond repair, you'll need to replace it with a new part. A cabinetmaker or woodcarver can make a new part for you. If you have an identical part still intact on the piece of furniture, take it to the cabinetmaker so that it can be duplicated. For more complicated replacement parts, take the whole piece of furniture.

Once you have a replacement part, refer to the appropriate section in this chapter and place the new piece according to the directions. Be sure to review the rules for gluing (page 44).

4. STRIPPING

TYPE OF FINISH	STRIPPING AGENT
Lacquer, shellac	Lacquer solvent, *Acetone*, Howard's Strip-a-Finish, paint remover (page 73)
Varnish, paint, linseed oil finish, polyurethane	Paint remover (page 75)

WHAT FINISH REMOVERS TO USE

The type of *finish* on a piece of furniture determines what removing agent you should use. Finishes fall basically into two categories: those removed by paint remover only and those which can be removed by paint remover as well as the other *solvents* listed below. Paint removers are the strongest removing agents and should only be used when a milder solvent won't strip the finish.

If you're not sure what kind of finish your furniture has, try dissolving some of whatever it is with acetone (fingernail polish remover) or lacquer solvent. If either of these remove the finish, it's lacquer or shellac. If not, it's varnish, linseed oil, paint, or polyurethane, and you'll have to use paint remover.

REMOVING CLEAR FINISHES (SHELLAC AND LACQUER)

Removers listed for shellac and lacquer are known as *clear-finish removers* or *clear strippers*. The following directions can be used for any of the removers listed. These clear strippers are generally a clear liquid solvent.

MATERIALS

Clear-finish stripper
(lacquer solvent,
Howard's Strip-a-Finish, acetone)
Rags
Steel wool (grade 0000)
Paint brush
Coffee can or jar

1. Generously paint the stripper onto the surface. Continue adding more liquid if it dries—the surface should be uniformly wet.

2. Leave the stripper on for approximately 10 minutes.

3. Scrub with grade-0000 steel wool in the direction of the grain.

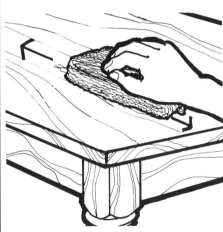

4. Wipe with a clean cloth.

Repeat steps 1–4 a second or even a third time if all of the finish does not come off the first time. (It rarely does.) Wait longer for the liquid to dissolve the finish before wiping it off.

No rinse or neutralizer is necessary before staining. Clear-finish strippers evaporate quickly—in 10 to 15 minutes. As soon as the piece is dry it can be stained.

Stripper chemicals work best on a dry surface. Wait for the surface to dry completely between applications.

Be careful! The vapors from stripping agents are very toxic. Use stripping agents only in a well-ventilated area, preferably out-of-doors.

PAINT REMOVERS (FOR STRIPPING
PAINT AND PAINT-BASE FINISHES)

Be sure to read the directions on the
paint remover you select. There are
two types of paint remover:

1. *Liquid removers* are usually
cheaper, but they evaporate quickly
and you have to work fast.

2. *Paste-type removers* (thickened
liquid removers) are generally easier
to use and more efficient because
they evaporate slowly and do not
run off easily. I recommend this
type.

The following directions are for
paste-type removers. **Be sure to
wear heavy rubber gloves—these
chemicals will burn your skin!**

MATERIALS

Paste-type paint remover

Container—glass or metal
(plastic will dissolve)

Paint brush
(one you can throw away)

Broad knife or putty knife

Orange stick—for carved areas

Wire brush
(with wooden handle)

Steel wool (grades 1 and 0000)

Paint thinner

1. With the paint brush apply the
paste-type remover liberally to the
surface: paint it on with a single
motion—don't brush back and forth
over the remover, as this will cause
evaporation as the solvent is
released and will weaken the
remover's effectiveness.

2. Leave the remover on the surface
the maximum time prescribed in the
remover directions. When the paint
has bubbled and lifted, scrape it off.
A wire brush, grade 1 steel wool,
and a broad knife with round edges
can be used to scrape off the finish.

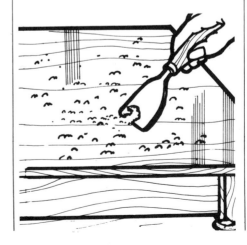

Round off edges of the broad knife with a metal file to prevent gouging the surface as you scrape off the dissolved paint or finish.

3. After scraping off as much finish as possible, rinse with paint thinner and wipe clean with rags and grade 0000 steel wool.

Don't wash the wood with water even if the remover directions say to. Water raises the grain of the wood, and then you'll have to do a lot of sanding before applying a new finish. Another disadvantage of rinsing with water is that you have to wait until the piece is completely dry before repeating the stripping process or staining or finishing. Paint thinner dries in 10 to 15 minutes, and you can begin the next process.

If there are still traces of finish left after the piece is dry, repeat steps 1–3.

Be careful! The vapors from paint thinner and paint remover are very toxic. Work only in a well-ventilated area, preferably out-of-doors.

If the finish is coming off slowly, try letting the solvent stay on longer. If this doesn't help, try another brand of remover.

CARVED AREAS

For removing paint, *varnish,* or linseed oil from heavily carved areas, put on the *paste-type remover* and leave it on for the maximum time given in the remover directions. When the *finish* has lifted, scrape it off with a toothbrush, *orange stick,** manicure tools, or dental tools.

*See list of sources.

5. BLEACHING

WOOD SURFACE	TYPE OF BLEACH
Dark spots, marks (such as ink)	Laundry bleach (page 79) or *oxalic acid* (page 81)
Original *stain*	*Two-step bleach* (page 84)
Natural wood color	*Two-step bleach* (page 84)

WHEN TO BLEACH

Bleaching can be used to take out spots and marks or to remove color from the wood for a new lighter hue or in preparation for restaining.

Bleaching can only be done to stripped or raw wood. Bleach will not penetrate a finish. After the piece has been bleached it can be stained, sealed, and finished.

LAUNDRY BLEACH

Laundry bleach (sodium hypochlorite) is the weakest of the bleaches listed in the chart. It's probably the bleaching agent you're most likely to have around the house, so try it first to remove spots. All laundry bleaches are sodium hypochlorite, so buy the cheapest brand. If the spots are on finished wood, it must be stripped first.

MATERIALS

Laundry bleach

Old paint brush (about 2″ wide)

Coffee can or jar

Rags

Wet/dry sandpaper (grade 400)

Steel wool (grade 0000)

Paint thinner

Only stripped or raw wood can be bleached. Bleach will not penetrate finished wood.

1. Clean the entire surface to be bleached with paint thinner and steel wool. Allow to dry 10 to 15 minutes. (See cleaning, page 6.)

2. Pour about 1 cup of bleach into a container. Using an old paint brush, apply laundry bleach generously to the surface. Cover the entire surface so that it will bleach uniformly. Don't let the bleach drip down onto other surfaces—it will cause discoloration.

3. If bleach is not readily absorbed into the wood, work it in with the grade 0000 steel wool, *rubbing in the direction of the grain.*

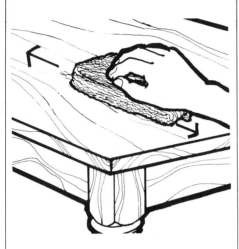

4. Laundry bleach works *immediately* if it's going to work at all. Leave the bleach on the wood from 2 to 4 minutes and wipe it off with rags.

5. After the wood is dry (4 to 5 hours), sand it with grade 400 wet/dry sandpaper

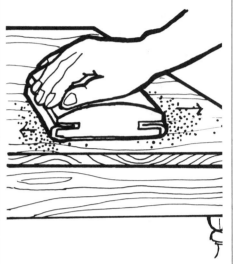

Now you're ready to *stain, seal,* and *finish* the surface (see pages 96, 102, and 110). If the laundry bleach didn't take out the spots, try bleaching with *oxalic acid* (see page 81).

OXALIC ACID

Oxalic acid, a crystallized salt, turns into bleach when dissolved in water. It can be bought in small quantities at drugstores or in large quantities at hardware stores. One piece of furniture needs only a few ounces.

MATERIALS

Oxalic acid

Old paint brush

Rags

Wet/dry sandpaper (grade 400)

Sudless ammonia:

Only stripped or raw wood can be bleached. Bleach will not penetrate finished wood.

1. Clean as described in cleaning (page 6). If possible, work in the sun to enhance the bleaching action.

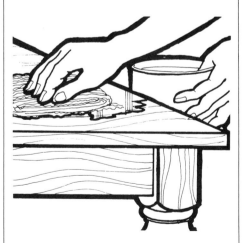

2. Dissolve 1 oz. oxalic acid crystals in 1 cup of hot water. The solution is now oxalic bleach. It may be heated to make it more effective.

3. Using a paint brush, apply the oxalic bleach to *entire surface* to be bleached.

4. If the oxalic bleach is not readily absorbed into the wood, work it in with grade 0000 steel wool, *rubbing in the direction of the grain.*

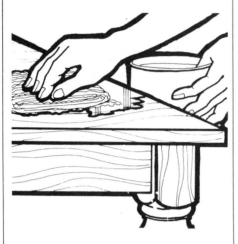

5. Allow the wood to dry completely - about 1 hour

Oxalic bleach continues to work while it is wet. If the stain isn't completely removed with the first application, apply a second coat and allow it also to dry. This can be done as many times as necessary. If you're bleaching veneer, watch carefully while it is damp. If it starts to lift or become loose in any way, dry the surface with rags immediately. (See repairing loose inlay or veneer, page 35.) Don't let the bleach drip onto other surfaces—it will cause discoloration.

6. When the surface has been completely bleached and the bleach has dried, there will be a residue of oxalic crystals that must be neutralized.

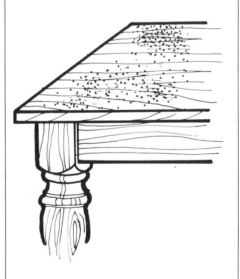

7. Be careful not to breathe the crystal residue on the wood.
Prepare a neutralizing solution of 1 cup of sudless ammonia and 2 quarts of water. Wash the entire surface with the solution. Wipe dry with rags.

8. Let the wood dry for approximately 5 hours before you start to seal, stain, and finish the surface.

Be careful not to breathe the oxalic bleach residue that has dried on the wood. It's highly irritating to the nose and throat. Wear a handkerchief or surgical mask over your nose and mouth while you're washing the crystals off or sanding the surface. The oxalic acid in water does not create irritating fumes.

Oxalic acid

TWO-STEP BLEACHES

Two-step bleaches are commercial preparations sold in hardware stores for removing *stains* and the natural color of the wood. They are the most powerful of the bleaching chemicals. If they don't take out the stain, nothing will. Follow the directions on the package carefully.

The following are general directions that can be used with any of the two-step bleaches. However, be sure to read the directions on the bleach, as they may vary from brand to brand.

MATERIALS

Two-step wood bleach
(such as Nutone or Jasco)

Old paint brush

Coffee can or jar

Rags

Steel wool (grade 1)

Lacquer thinner

Wet/dry sandpaper (grade 400)

Only stripped or raw wood can be bleached. Bleach will not penetrate finished wood. Follow the manufacturer's instructions.

1. Clean the piece of furniture as described in cleaning (page 6).

2. With the paint brush, apply the chemical labeled #1. Leave it on the surface for the amount of time specified in the directions— generally 10 to 20 minutes. This allows the chemical to penetrate the wood.

3. Apply the chemical labeled #2. Leave it on the surface for the amount of time in the instructions. The two chemicals will react and take the color out of the wood, leaving a crusty film on the surface.

4. Once the reaction has finished, remove the film from the surface with steel wool and rags. If the crust doesn't come off easily, scrub it off with lacquer thinner and steel wool.

5. Let the piece dry thoroughly and sand it with grade 400 wet/dry sandpaper

The piece is now ready to be stained, sealed, and finished (see pages 96, 102, and 110).

6. SANDING

TYPES OF SANDPAPER

TYPE	USES AND CHARACTERISTICS
Flint or *sandpaper*	Rough sanding through many coats of paint; the grit clogs easily.
Garnet	Rough and medium sandings; clogs easily.
Alumium oxide; silicone carbide (wet/dry)*	Fine sanding; grit does not clog easily.

*These two sandpapers are recommended for refinishing jobs. Use grades 400 to 600.

WHEN AND HOW TO SAND

Sanding is an important step in refinishing. If the wood surface is uneven, the *stain* and *finish* coats will be uneven. Sanding should be done by hand, since sanding machines are difficult to control and can easily damage the surface. Furniture that is being refinished is generally smooth and needs only a finish sanding. If the *grain* has been raised from contact with water when it was stripped or bleached, the raised grain should be smoothed out by sanding.

BASIC RULES FOR SANDING

1. Use a *sanding block.*
2. Sand in the direction of the grain.
3. As you sand, keep the pressure uniform with each stroke.

MAKING AND USING SANDING BLOCKS

A *sanding block* is a flat block with sandpaper wrapped around it. The block allows even pressure to be applied to each stroke to produce a uniform satin smoothness. Sanding blocks can be purchased or you can make them yourself. The illustrations below show some blocks you can make or buy for sanding.

An essential element of the sanding block is a piece of some resilient material such as felt, rubber, or carpet between the block and the paper to prevent loose grit from getting between the block and the paper. A piece of grit stuck underneath the surface makes a bump in the sanding surface of the block, which will in turn cause gouges in the wood.

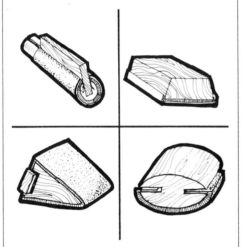

7. NEW AND UNPAINTED OR UNFINISHED FURNITURE

TREATING NEW, UNFINISHED,
UNPAINTED FURNITURE

If you have purchased or made a
new piece of furniture which is
unfinished, follow the directions in
the sections for sanding (page 88),
sealing (page 102), staining (page
96), and finishing (page 110).
Unpainted furniture is essentially
the same as a piece which has been
stripped. The only difference might
be that more sanding is necessary.
Furniture which was once finished
and has now been stripped was
originally given a fine-finish
sanding. A piece which you have
just constructed or bought
unpainted will require a fine-finish
sanding. Some manufacturers of
unpainted furniture do this before it
leaves the factory, but not all. If the
piece feels rough to the touch, it
needs more sanding.

FINE-FINISH SANDING

1. Using a sanding block and grade 280 wet/dry sandpaper, sand all rough areas.

2. Switch grade to 400 wet/dry sandpaper. Sand the entire piece until it is very smooth and satiny to the touch.

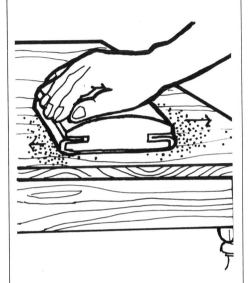

8. STAINING

Types of stain

TYPES OF STAIN

Stains are solvents mixed with color. Color is added by mixing in dyes or pigments. Dyes are transparent and pigments are opaque. If the stain you select is clear, the color in it is dye. If the stain is milky or opaque, the color added is pigment.

The clear (dye) stains are used for woods with a naturally beautiful grain. The dye stains darken the wood and define the grain. Pigment stains also do this, but the pigment tends to hide the grain somewhat, so these stains are used to camouflage poor woods or to achieve a uniform appearance on pieced-together woods. Most stains available in hardward stores are the pigment type. If you cannot obtain a dye stain and wish to avoid the camouflaging effect of pigment stains, do not mix the stain thoroughly. The pigment will settle to the bottom of the can but enough color will remain in the liquid to enhance the wood grain.

APPLICATION TECHNIQUES

The surface must be uniformly smooth, otherwise the stain will not penetrate evenly.

MATERIALS
Stain

Paint Brush

Rags

Solvent

Containers

Sandpaper

1. Before staining, clean the surface so that it's free of wax, dirt, and old finish. (See cleaning, page 6.)

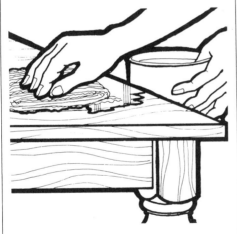

2. Work on a single surface at a time—back, sides, top, and so on. When possible, work on each surface in a horizontal position—that is, the surface of the furniture should be horizontal.

3. Where vertical surfaces are unavoidable, *work from bottom to top*. This prevents drips and overlap marks.

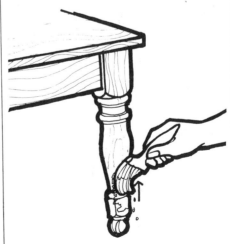

4. Apply the stain with a paint brush so that each succeeding stroke butts against the still-wet edges of the preceding stroke.

5. Wipe off excess stain with a rag. Use the rag to work the stain into the pores of the wood.

CHOOSING STAINS

The solvent used for stain is water, paint thinner, alcohol, *lacquer* thinner, or oil. *Do not use water-base stains—they will raise the grain.* Stains dissolved in paint thinner, lacquer thinner, and alcohol dry very quickly and therefore must be applied quickly to achieve a uniform look. Oil takes at least 24 hours to dry and can be applied slowly. Find out at the store where you purchase the stain what the base is.

Oil stains are easiest to use and are recommended for the beginner.

Hints:
Always test the color of the stain to be sure it's the color you want. Apply a small amount of the stain to an inconspicuous part of the furniture (the bottom of a chair, the inside of a leg). Let the stain dry to show its true color. (Refer to the stain label for drying time.) If you apply the stain and immediately notice that it's too dark, you can lighten it by wiping it with a rag dampened with solvent specified on the label.

9. SEALING

TYPE OF SEALER	USE
Paste wood filler	Seals wood with large pores, such as oak, and seals badly weathered woods (page 103).
Sealing stains—sometimes called wiping stains	Seals and colors wood at the same time; can be used alone or before other coats of finish (page 105).
Sanding sealer	Seals woods to be finished (page 107).

TYPES AND USES OF SEALERS

Sealers penetrate the surface fibers of the wood, giving it a tough, wearable surface—without a coating of film. Wood should always be sealed. This fills the pores and prevents warping, splitting, and drying.

Wood should be sealed even if it is not going to be finished, to protect against moisture and, if the wood is to be finished, to provide a smooth base surface.

PASTE WOOD FILLER

Paste wood filler is used to seal and fill the pores of badly weathered or extremely-open-grain woods.

MATERIALS

Paste wood filler
Old paint brush
Burlap
Wet/dry sandpaper (grade 400)
Coffee can or jar

1. Wood should be uniformly sanded, stained, and free of dust and dirt.

2. Apply the filler in broad, even strokes—first with the grain and then against the grain. Use an old paint brush to scrub the filler into the pores. Scrub in a circular direction to fill up the pores in the surface.

3. Let the filler dry about 2 hours. The surface will look dull when it's dry.

4. Using the burlap, rub off the excess filler.

5. Wipe the surface clean and allow it to dry for 24 hours.

6. Sand with grade 400 (or finer) wet/dry sandpaper.

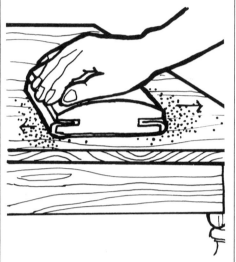

The wood is now ready to be stained and finished. (See staining, page 96, and finishing, page 110.)

SEALER STAINS

Sealer stains allow you to stain and seal the wood in one step. They produce an *oiled finish*, and another finish is not necessary if you want a no-gloss "country look" for the wood.

MATERIALS

Sealing stain
(usually oil-base)

Solvent (read stain label for type of solvent)

Paint brush

Tack rag

Rags

1. Wood should be uniformly sanded and free of dust and dirt.

2. Apply sealer stain to surface liberally. Leave it on the wood for 15 minutes while it is being absorbed, then wipe the excess stain off with rags.

3. Let dry for 24 hours.

4. Wipe with a tack rag to remove all particles of dust and dirt.

The wood can be left as is, or a finish can be applied. (See finishing, page 110.)

SANDING SEALERS

MATERIALS

Sanding sealer

Solvent (check sealer label for type of solvent)

Paint brush

Wet/dry sandpaper (grade 400 or finer)

Tack rag

Rags

1. Wood should be uniformly sanded, stained, and free of dust and dirt.

2. Paint on sanding sealer in even strokes with the grain.

3. Allow to dry for 24 hours.

4. Sand with grade-400 wet/dry sandpaper.

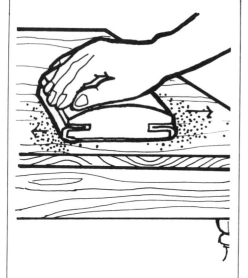

5. Clean off dust with rags and a tack rag.

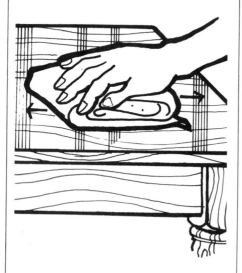

Now the wood is ready for a coat of finish. (See finishing, page 110.)

10. FINISHING

FINISH	DURABILITY	DRYING TIME
Shellac	Somewhat durable	Dries rapidly
Lacquer	Durable	Dries rapidly
Varnish	Very durable	24 hours
Polyurethane	Most durable	24 hours

TYPES OF FINISHES

A *finish* is a liquid coating that forms a protective film over the surface of the wood. Finishes are sold in semi-gloss, *satin*, or *high-gloss*.

For special finishes, see high-gloss or piano finish (page 116), antiquing (page 117), and pickling (page 120).

Shellac **should be purchased in small quantities because it spoils. Once opened, shellac absorbs moisture from the air and will dry cloudy. Always use a new container of shellac.**

SPRAY-ON TECHNIQUE (LACQUER, VARNISH, OR POLYURETHANE)

A sprayed-on *finish* yields a more even coat and dries faster than a brushed-on finish. Few dust particles get trapped in the finish during the short drying period, and there are no brush marks or loose bristles left in the finish.

Select *flat, satin,* or *high-gloss* in *lacquer, varnish,* or *polyurethane* finish. If you're using a spray gun, follow the manufacturer's directions; the general procedure is the same as for aerosol cans.

MATERIALS:

Finish of your choice

Spray gun
(for nonaerosol finishes)

Solvent (read finish label
for solvent)

Wet/dry sandpaper (grade 600)

Tack rags

Rags

1. The wood should first be stained (page 96), sealed (page 102), and sanded (page 88).

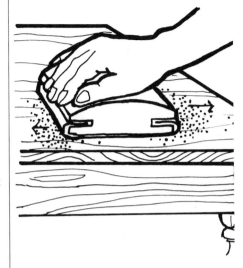

2. Make sure the surface is free of dust and dirt (see cleaning, page 6). Work in a dust-free area. Wipe the entire piece with a tack rag.

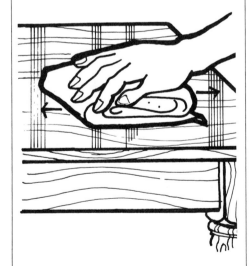

3. Shake the spray gun (or aerosol can) vigorously.

4. Check the nozzle by spraying in the air—you should get a fine mist of spray.

5. Apply a very thin coat of lacquer by spraying the entire surface with an even, circular motion.

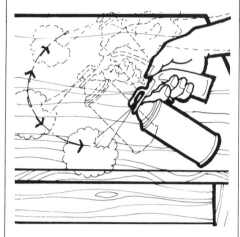

6. After spraying, clear the nozzle by turning the gun or can upside down and depressing the spray valve until only air comes out. This keeps the nozzle from clogging.

7. Allow the finish to dry (refer to the finish label for drying time). Lacquer usually dries in 15 minutes.

8. When dry, sand ("rub out") with grade 600 wet/dry sandpaper. Use a sanding block to sand (see page 89), applying uniform pressure and *sanding in the direction of the grain.*

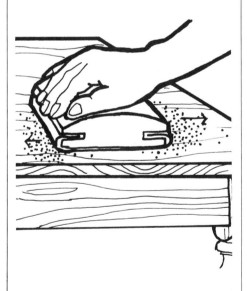

9. Clean dust from the surface with rags and tack rags.

10. Apply a second coat as outlined in steps 3–8. Allow the finish to dry for 24 hours.

If a duller look is desired, rub out the final coat with grade 600 wet/dry sandpaper.

BRUSH-ON TECHNIQUE (LACQUER, VARNISH, OR POLYURETHANE)

It's more difficult to achieve a uniformly smooth finish when applying a *finish* with a brush rather than a spray gun or aerosol can. However, if you insist on brushing (some people find it therapeutic), these are the directions to follow.

MATERIALS:

*Finish** of your choice (*lacquer* must be brushing lacquer)

Solvent (read finish label for solvent)

New paint brush (preferably china bristle)

Wet/dry sandpaper (grade 600)

Tack rags

Rags

1. The wood should first be stained (page 96), sealed (page 102), and sanded (page 88).

2. Make sure the surface is free of dust and dirt (see cleaning, page 6). Try to work in a dust-free area. Wipe the entire piece with a tack rag.

3. Apply the finish with a paint brush in even strokes with the grain. Keep the brush loaded with finish, so that it flows on evenly. Brush in one direction. *Avoid brushing areas twice.*

*See types of finishes (page 110).

4. Let the finish dry. Drying time varies with the finish, so follow the instructions on the can. Don't worry about small brushstrokes—they can be sanded (rubbed) out.

5. When dry, sand ("rub out") with grade 600 wet/dry sandpaper. Use a sanding block (page 89) for uniform pressure, and *sand in the direction of the grain.*

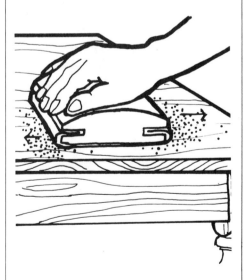

6. Clean dust from the surface with rags and tack rags.

7. Apply a second coat as in steps 3–6. Allow to dry for 24 hours

If a dull finish is desired, rub out the final coat with grade 600 wet/dry sandpaper.

HIGH-GLOSS OR PIANO FINISH

High-gloss finish ("piano finish") is a very shiny (reflective) finish which is achieved by rubbing out many successive coats of *lacquer* with *rottenstone*, a fine abrasive powder, mixed with oil.

MATERIALS

*Rottenstone**

Paraffin oil (actually, any oil is suitable for suspending the rottenstone)

Felt square†

Paint thinner cloths

Follow the directions for applying a lacquer finish (page 111 or 114).

l. After each coat of lacquer is dry, use the felt square to rub it out with rottenstone mixed in paraffin oil. Mix the oil and rottenstone together to form a paste about the consistency of peanut butter.

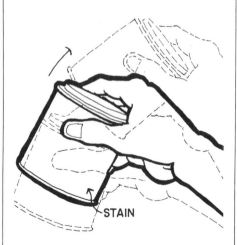

STAIN

2. Clean the surface thoroughly with paint thinner and cloths.

3. Apply another coat of finish (see page 111 or 114). Repeat steps 1–3 until the finish has the lustre and depth you want. (It will take at least five coats.)

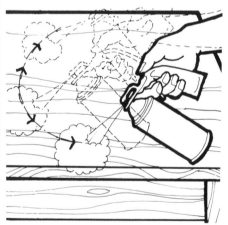

*Rottenstone is a very fine abrasive powder that "sands" down the finish evenly.
† Use an 8′ × 12″ inch piece of felt, folded in fourths, for rubbing on the rottenstone-oil mixture.

ANTIQUING

The *antiquing* process involves a painted finish with a glaze coat that gives an aged look. Antiquing is a popular way to finish French-style furniture.

MATERIALS

Flat or glossy enamel
(oil- or latex-base
enamel paint)—the base color

Glaze (½ cup *varnish* + 1 teaspoon burnt sienna oil color or UTC
— or store-bought glaze)

Gold enamel paint
(if gilding is desired)

Cheesecloth or terrycloth

Paint brush

Cotton swabs

1. The wood should be sanded (page 88) and free of dust and dirt (see cleaning, page 6).

2. If gilding is desired, paint on gold paint in the areas you wish to accent—carvings, grooves, and so on.

3. Allow the paint to dry for 24 hours.

4. Paint the entire surface with the base-color paint.

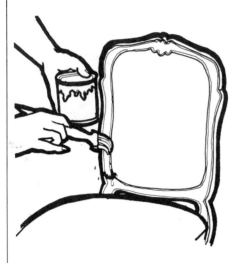

5. If you've used the gold paint first, while the base color is still wet wipe off accent areas with cotton swabs so that a small amount of gold shows through.

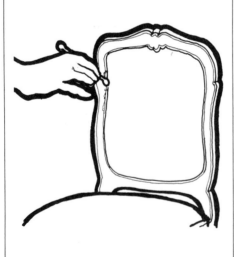

6. Allow the base coat to dry, following the instructions on the paint can for drying time. Generally you will have to wait 24 hours for paint to dry.

7. Dip a cloth into the glaze and wipe it on, wiping with the grain. If a darker look is desired, wipe the glaze on a second time.

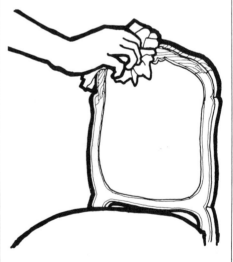

8. Allow to dry for 24 hours.

PICKLING

Pickling produces a two-tone finish with a lighter color rubbed into the pores of the wood and a darker glaze coating on the surface. The grain of the wood is visible.

MATERIALS

Gesso (buy it premixed)

Paint brush

Rags

Boiled linseed oil

Oil color—raw sienna

Container

Toothbrush

Lacquer

Wet/dry sandpaper (grade 280)

1. The wood should be sanded (page 88) and free of dust and dirt (see cleaning, page 6).

2. Paint on the gesso with a brush. Wipe off the excess with a rag.

3. Allow the gesso to dry—about 5 hours.

4. Sand the gesso with grade 280 wet/dry sandpaper.

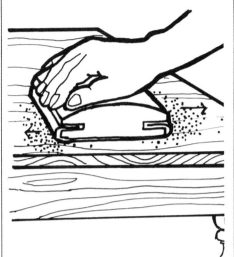

5. Mix oil color (raw sienna) with boiled linseed oil: use ½ cup boiled linseed oil and ½ teaspoon color.

6. Using the rag, wipe on the oil mixture.

7. Dip the toothbrush in the glaze (in the can) and flick it on the glazed surface so that the spattered droplets create a "wormhole" effect.

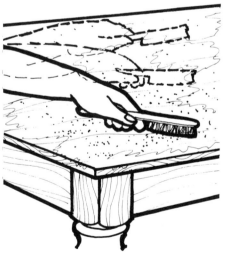

8. Allow the surface to dry for 24 hours.

9. Coat with lacquer to seal and protect the pickled finish. (See the spray-on or brush-on technique sections, pages 111 and 114, respectively.)

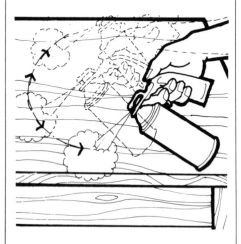

For additional aging effect, gesso and color can be applied more heavily in areas that receive more wear, such as the edges of doors, handles, and drawers.

BOILED LINSEED OIL FINISH

Boiled linseed is an oil that dries slowly (sometimes a week or more) and forms a hard *varnish*-like film. This finish is often found on American oak furniture.

MATERIALS

Boiled linseed oil

Rags

Tack rag

Paint brush

Container

1. The wood should first be stained (page 96), sealed (page 102), and sanded (page 88).

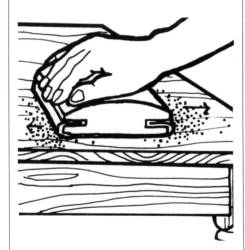

2. Make sure the surface is free of dust and dirt (see cleaning, page 6). Work in a dirt-free area. Wipe the entire piece with a tack rag.

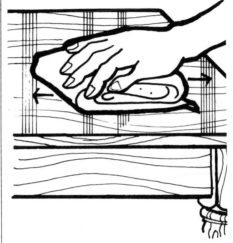

3. Apply linseed oil liberally to the surface of the furniture with a paint brush.

4. Allow oil to sit on the surface for 15 minutes.

5. Wipe the surface dry with rags.

6. Allow to dry for at least 24 hours or as long as necessary.

OILED FINISH

An *oiled finish* produces a natural look and is often used on teak, walnut, and oak. This *finish* is achieved by sealing the wood with an oil sealer or an oil sealer-stain. (See sealing, page 102.) If the finish on an oiled piece of furniture begins to look dry, apply a furniture oil such as lemon oil to the surface.

Oiled finish

GLOSSARY

ACETONE: A liquid solvent used in removing lacquer and shellac finishes.

ACRYLIC PAINTS: Water-base paints used by artists. Similar to oil paints. These paints are generally sold in tubes.

ANTIQUING: A painted finish that is glazed to give the appearance of a very old painted finish.

BOILED LINSEED OIL: An oil which when applied to wood surfaces dries into a varnish-like finish. Originally raw linseed oil was actually boiled to give it this drying quality. Today, driers such as Japan driers are added to the oil to make it dry.

BUILD: A layer of sealer that fills up small pores in wood surfaces and provides a uniform surface on which to apply successive coats of finish.

C-CLAMPS: A vise-like clamp in the shape of the letter "C." (See illustration, page 46.)

CLEAR FINISH REMOVER: A clear liquid solvent used to remove finishes such as lacquer and shellac. Most clear finish removers are predominantly composed of acetone.

DOWELS: Cylindrical wooden sticks available in diameters from ¼ to 1¼", approximately.

DUCT TAPE: Silver-gray tape used to wrap heating ducts. It has a very strong adhesive quality.

FINISH: A liquid coating that forms a protective film over wood surfaces. Common finishes are lacquer, shellac, and polyurethane, and all are sold in high-gloss (very shiny, mirrorlike finish), semi-gloss or satin (medium shine), and flat gloss (low-luster finish sometimes referred to as hand-rubbed).

FLAT FINISH: A low-luster finish with no reflective qualities.

GARNET PAPER: Inexpensive sandpaper generally used for rough sanding jobs.

GESSO: A water-soluble, white, plaster-like substance sold in powder and pre-mixed forms.

GLUE (White): Water-soluble glue that dries transparent. Some popular brands are Elmer's, Glu-Bird, Wilhold, and Weldwood.

GRAIN: The arrangement of fibers, layers, and particles of wood.

HIGH-GLOSS: A finish of very shiny luster.

INLAY: Decorative patterns of small pieces of wood set into the surface of a base wood; also known as marquetry and parquetry. Marquetry is fashioned in floral patterns; parquetry is geometrical.

LACQUER: A clear synthetic or resinous coating used to give wood a high-gloss, medium-gloss, or flat finish. It is best applied by spraying, using a spray gun or aerosol can.

LIQUID REMOVER: Substances which remove clear finishes.

OIL-BASE PAINT: Pigment added to an oil base. Paint thinner must be used for cleanup and as a solvent.

OIL-BASE STAIN: Color in the form of dye or pigment suspended in oil and used to stain wood.

OILED FINISH: A natural looking finish often used on teak, walnut, and oak. Achieved by sealing the wood with an oil sealer or an oil sealer-stain.

OIL PAINTS: Oil-base paints sold in tubes for use by artists.

ORANGE STICK: A wooden stick with pointed ends used by manicurists.

OXALIC ACID: A white crystalline substance. Acts as a bleach when dissolved in water.

PASTE-TYPE PAINT REMOVER: A thick liquid that dissolves shellac, lacquer, varnish, paint, and linseed oil finishes.

PASTE WOOD FILLER: Thick substance (peanut butter consistency) used to fill pores in the surfaces of wide-grained or badly-weathered woods. Provides a smooth surface on which to apply finishes.

PATINA: The color change caused by aging in wood. The natural process of oxidation creates shading and tones that lend character, depth, and beauty to wood. Stripping removes most of the patina.

PICKLING: A decorator finish applied in two steps. First, the pores of the wood are filled with a light color (usually white). Then a darker glaze is applied to the entire wood surface.

POLYURETHANE: A clear, hard, abrasion- and chemical-resistant finish. Generally it is used only on pieces of furniture that constantly come in contact with water (bars, restaurant tables, wood in a bathroom, children's furniture). It dries slowly and tends to collect dust as it dries, making it difficult to achieve a smooth, flawless finish.

RAW LINSEED OIL: A pure organic oil which does not dry.

ROTTENSTONE: A very fine abrasive powder that is mixed with oil and used to buff or "sand' the finish smooth, especially in very-high-gloss (piano finish) applications.

SANDING BLOCK: A flat block with sandpaper wrapped around it. The block allows even pressure with each stroke to produce a uniform smoothness.

SANDING SEALER: A liquid that is painted on the wood surfaces, allowed to dry, and then sanded. It penetrates the surface fibers of wood, resulting in a tough, wearable surface.

SANDPAPER: (Wet/dry): Silicone carbide sandpaper is generally referred to as wet/dry (or wet-and-dry) sandpaper because it can be used with a lubricant (wet) or without (dry). It does not fall apart when used with liquids such as paint thinner, water, or oil. It is also a nonload paper, which means the grit does not become clogged while sanding.

SATIN: A finish of medium luster, also referred to as a semi-gloss finish.

SEALER: A chemical that penetrates the surface fibers of wood, giving the wood a tough, wearable surface.

SEALER STAIN: A stain mixed with chemicals that seal the surface fibers of wood.

SEMI-GLOSS: A finish of medium luster or shine (satin gloss).

SHELLAC: A liquid finish that forms a protective film over the surface of wood.

SHIMS: Pieces of wood such as slivers, toothpicks, or matchsticks, or cloth, used as filler in securing loose joints.

SOLVENT: A substance which will dissolve another.

SPLINE: A small piece of wood used to fill cracks and crevices in furniture surfaces.

STAIN: Color mixed with oil, alcohol, water, or other liquids and absorbed by wood. Stain deepens and enhances the contrast of the grain and adds color.

STEEL WOOL: An abrasive pad of steel threads. You can buy it in various grades—the smaller the number, the finer the wool: #3 is coarse, #0 is fine, #0000 is very fine.

STRETCHER: The rungs between the legs of a chair. They strengthen and help support the chair legs.

TACK RAG: A cloth treated with a gummy substance, used to remove the last traces of dust and dirt before applying a coat of finish.

TWO-STEP BLEACH: A peroxide wood bleach consisting of two liquids that are applied to wood surfaces. Liquid #1 is painted on the surface of the wood and allowed to penetrate, and liquid #2 is painted on the surface. When liquids #1 and #2 are combined, they become a bleach.

UTC: Universal Tinting Colors—
pigments used to color many
substances. They can be mixed with
oil, water, paint, varnish, or lacquer.

VARNISH: A resinous liquid
substance used to give a glossy
finish to wood.

VENEER: A thin surface layer of
wood, 1/32 to 1/64″ thick, usually of
finer quality than the base wood to
which it is glued.

WAX STICKS (hard and soft): Hard
wax sticks are sold in wood-tone
colors and are melted to fill small
holes and gouges. Soft wax sticks
are also sold in wood colors and can
be rubbed directly into scratches.

WOOD PUTTY (also called wood
dough or plastic wood): A synthetic,
doughy clay that dries with a hard,
woodlike texture. It is sold in small
cans in a variety of wood-tone
colors. It is also sold in neutral
shades that can be colored to match
any wood.

SOURCES

Almost all the materials in this book are available at hardware stores, home improvement centers, and art supply stores. You'll find most materials produced by several different companies, but some are specialty items, available from one or only a few manufacturers. Such items are listed alphabetically below, with the addresses of their suppliers.

GLUE SYRINGE: an injector device with a fine-point tip for shooting glue into hard-to-reach places. Available through Albert Constantine & Sons, Inc., 2050 Eastchester Road, New York, NY 10461. Phone: (212) 792-1600.

HARDWARE, DUPLICATING: Ritter and Son will duplicate old hardware. To get an estimate of the duplicating cost, send one of the original pieces of hardware. They also manufacture a large selection of reproduction hardware, mostly in American Victorian style. Send for a catalog of styles to Ritter and Son, P.O. Box 907, Campbell, CA 95008. Phone: (408) 378-3272.

HOWARD'S PRODUCTS: Howard's Restor-a-Finish is a stainlike treatment for removing white water spots and camouflaging scratches in the finish.

Howard's Strip-a-Finish is a clear finish stripper used to remove lacquer and shellac finishes. It works quickly, does not require a neutralizer, does not burn the skin, and does not raise the grain of the wood.

Howard's manufactures an excellent line of finishing products. Write for a free brochure describing all of their products: Howard's Products, Inc., P.O. Box 641, Sierra Madre, CA 91024.

ORANGE STICKS: thin wood sticks used by manicurists. They have a pencil point at one end and a tapered, rounded point at the other end and are available in diameters from 1/8 to 3/8". They make excellent tools for removing paint from carved areas: because they are wood they do not scratch as pointed metal tools can. Orange sticks are sold by beauty supply houses or in the cosmetic departments of drugstores and department stores.

OXALIC ACID: a crystalline, water-soluble substance for bleaching. It can be purchased in small quantities (2 to 4 oz.) at most pharmacies. Ask your druggist. Some paint stores also sell oxalic acid.

VENEER AND INLAY: Most large lumberyards carry a line of veneer woods. They can also be ordered from Albert Constantine & Son, Inc., 2050 Eastchester Road, New York, NY 10461. Phone: (212) 792-1600.

Write for a free catalog of Constantine's many products, including decorative moldings and trim; carving, veneering, and other woodworking tools; finishing supplies; wood picture kits; hardware; and books on refinishing, woodworking, and wood.

INDEX

Index

141